OTHER BOOKS BY HARISH JOHARI

Tools for Tantra

Chakras
Energy Centers of Transformation

The Planet Meditation Kit

Numerology with Tantra, Ayurveda, and Astrology

Breath, Mind, and Consciousness

Ayurvedic Healing Cuisine
200 Vegetarian Recipes for Health, Balance, and Longevity

Ayurvedic Massage
Traditional Indian Techniques for Balancing Body and Mind

The Healing Power of Gemstones
In Tantra, Ayurveda, and Astrology

The Yoga of Snakes and Arrows
The Leela of Self-Knowledge

Dhanwantari
A Complete Guide to the Ayurvedic Life

The Monkeys and the Mango Tree

How Ganesh Got His Elephant Head
(with Vatsala Sperling)

How Parvati Won the Heart of Shiva
(with Vatsala Sperling)

Ganga
The River that Flows from Heaven to Earth
(Illustrator with Pieter Weltevrede, text by Vatsala Sperling)

Attunements for Dawn and Dusk (Audio)

Sounds of Tantra (Audio)

Sounds of the Chakras (Audio)

SPIRITUAL TRADITIONS
OF INDIA
COLORING BOOK

From the collected works of author and artist

HARISH JOHARI

Destiny Books
Rochester, Vermont • Toronto, Canada

Destiny Books
One Park Street
Rochester, Vermont 05767
www.DestinyBooks.com

Destiny Books is a division of Inner Traditions International

Library of Congress Cataloging-in-Publication Data available upon request.

ISBN 978-1-62055-629-0

Printed and bound in India by Replika Press Pvt., Ltd.

10 9 8 7 6 5 4 3 2 1

Text design and layout by Virginia Scott Bowman
This book was typeset in Garamond Premier Pro with Kolo used as the display typeface

CONTENTS

ABOUT THE AUTHOR
AND THE ILLUSTRATIONS

Harish Johari (1934–1999) was a distinguished North Indian author, Tantric scholar, gemologist, poet, musician, composer, painter, and sculptor who held degrees in philosophy and literature and made it his life's work to introduce the culture of his homeland to the West. He authored twelve books on Eastern spirituality, including *Tools for Tantra, Chakras, Numerology, The Planet Meditation Kit,* and *Ayurvedic Healing Cuisine.*

The painting tradition founded by Harish is a combination of the overall spiritual Indian art traditions and the special wash painting technique that he learned from his teacher Shri Chandra Bal, who himself learned it from Shri Bhawani Prasad Mittal, who learned it at Shanti Niketan. Johari's unique style is reflected throughout these pages in the images created by him and his students, Sandeep Johari, Pieter Weltevrede, and Jeanet Hazenberg.

The style of the figures is a mixture of three existing forms of Indian artwork that can be found in the painted or sculptured art forms in temples throughout India.

The faces—specifically the eyes, nose, and lips—and the hands and feet are drawn in the style of the paintings located in the Ajanta caves. They represent a two-thousand-year-old fresco style of artwork.

The proportions used in the figures are like those of the sculptures in the Elephanta caves near Bombay. These proportions were chosen because they are so beautiful and delicate, unlike the proportions found in the Ajanta cave paintings, which are very heavy and result in dwarflike figures. The sculptures in the Elephanta caves represent a style that is thousands of years older than the familiar Rajasthan style of artwork that is generally recognized as Indian art.

The postures are inspired by the ancient sculptures of the Ellora caves and the Khajoraho temple because of the grace, preciseness, and expressiveness that these sculptures exemplify.

Another important feature of the artwork is the rich use of hand postures. There are not more than ten hand postures that are generally drawn by artists throughout the world. Indian art, however, uses as many as sixty-four hand postures, reflecting the sixty-four hand postures used in Indian dance rituals and worship. These hand postures, or mudras, have their own symbolism and language and are used as a way to express emotions. The richness that is found in the hand postures of Indian art is a gift to the entire world. The artwork uses these hand postures as a language of the heart as opposed to the language of the head.

The images can evoke spiritual feelings in the viewers, while for those that use the illustrations as objects of meditation, the images can become a vehicle for spiritual contact with the divine beings.

As Harish said of the subjects of Indian spiritual art, "science is very beautifully explained in Indian iconography; the entire science of physics, the science of psychology, the science of sociology, interpersonal relationships . . . all these things are interwoven in Indian painting and in mythology."

ABOUT THE MANTRAS

Prayer and meditation are time-tested devices for changing a body's metabolism and creating a favorable balance of energy for living a happy, healthy, and inspired life. Mantras are composed of psychically potent sound syllables that resonate in our brains and influence our bodies. After reciting a mantra out loud, the same mantra can be repeated in silent *japa* (the act of repeating a mantra a specified number of times). Audible chanting will resonate mentally after the actual chanting has stopped and will repeat in the mind, usually resulting in either deep meditation or a creative rush of thought.

Mantra practice involves the left hemisphere of the brain and is therefore effective in increasing positive emotions and removing negative ones. In association with a yantra—a diagram or a picture of a deity—the mantra also provides the right hemisphere with a concrete image of the object of emotional attachment.

The practice of mantra is more than just a suggestion to the mind, a bit of advice, or an idea. It is a means of getting in touch with our Self.

Gods and Goddesses Mantras: The majority of the mantras found in this section are Gayatri Mantras, which are composed of twenty-four syllables. Each sound-syllable is the energy of any one of the twenty-four gods, and Gayatri is the combined force of these twenty-four different energies. Each energy is of a different nature and serves a different purpose. Doing japa of the chosen mantra daily can help in obtaining the desired energy.

The Chakra Mantras: Each chakra has a primary seed sound, or Bija Mantra, along with a seed sound for each petal. These mantras are sound frequencies used to invoke the divine energy inside the body. The seed sounds are supposed to contain great power and to aid in entering a state of deep uninterrupted concentration. Bija Mantras may or may not convey a direct translatable meaning, but their sounds are forms of the particular god, goddess, or chakra they represent.

The Yantra Mantras: Most of the yantras in this section are representative of one of the ten Mahavidyas and include the mantra of that goddess. The Mahavidyas are ten forms of the Divine Mother. Whenever some force creates imbalance or disharmony, the Divine Mother appears in some form to destroy that force and establish harmony and balance. Meditation on the Mahavidyas creates new knowledge and new dimensions of being.

The Planet Mantras: Designed to help us overcome disharmonies and mental and physical problems created by the negative or overpowering planet energies, the planet mantras help create balance and serenity, improving and strengthening your physical, mental, and spiritual health. The energy of each planet is best reached by meditation on that planet's day of the week: Sun–Sunday, Moon–Monday, Mars–Tuesday, Mercury–Wednesday, Jupiter–Thursday, Venus–Friday, Saturn–Saturday, Rahu–Sunday, Ketu–also Monday. These meditations can be followed by meditating on other planets whose energies you feel you need to put in better balance in your life. Planets do not force us to be any particular way; it is our own growth and development that determines our receptivity to the planetary energy.

Ganesha

Parvati and Shiva

Ram

Krishna

Hanuman

Durga

*Kamla
(Lakshmi)*

*Mantagi
(Saraswati)*

Kali

*Tripur Sundari
(Shri/Shodashi)*

*Ganga, born from
the divine energy
of Lord Vishnu,
daughter of
Lord Brahma*

*Kameshvara and
Kameshvari*

GODS
AND
GODDESSES

Ganesh Gayatri:
For removing obstacles

ॐ
एकदन्ताय विद्महे,
वक्रतुण्डाय धीमहि।
तन्नो बुद्धिः प्रचोदयात्॥

AUM EIKDANTAYE VIDMAHE,
VAKRATUNAYE DHI-MAHI
TAN NO BUDDHIH PRACHODAYAT

Ganesha

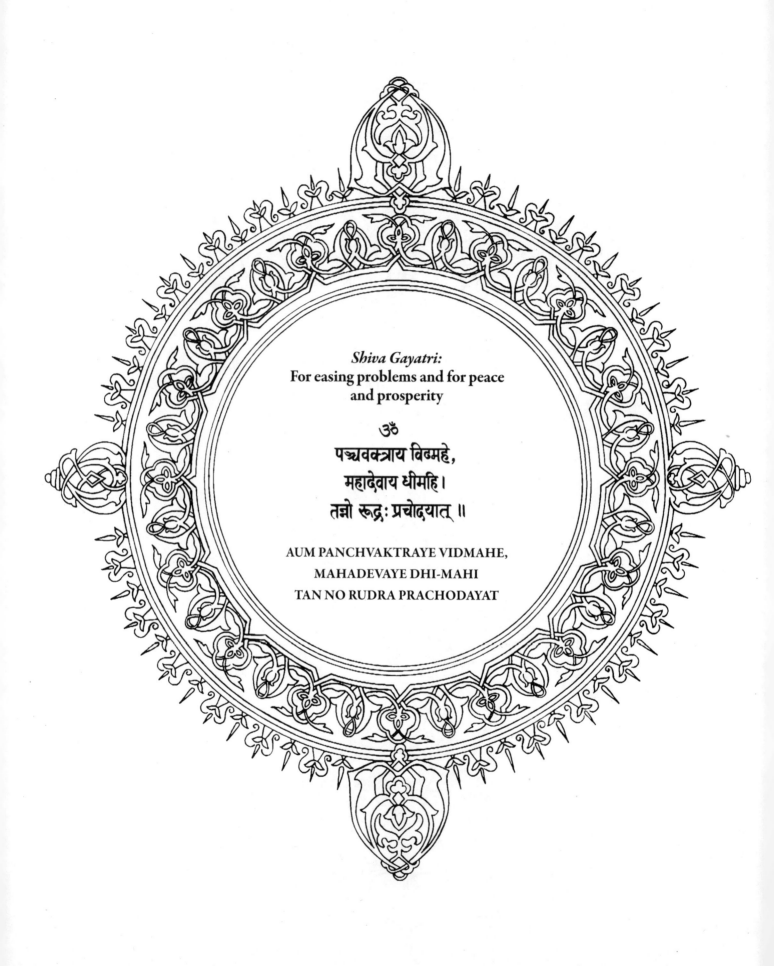

Shiva Gayatri:
**For easing problems and for peace
and prosperity**

ॐ

पञ्चवक्त्राय विद्महे,
महादेवाय धीमहि।
तन्नो रुद्रः प्रचोदयात् ॥

AUM PANCHVAKTRAYE VIDMAHE,
MAHADEVAYE DHI-MAHI
TAN NO RUDRA PRACHODAYAT

Parvati and Shiva

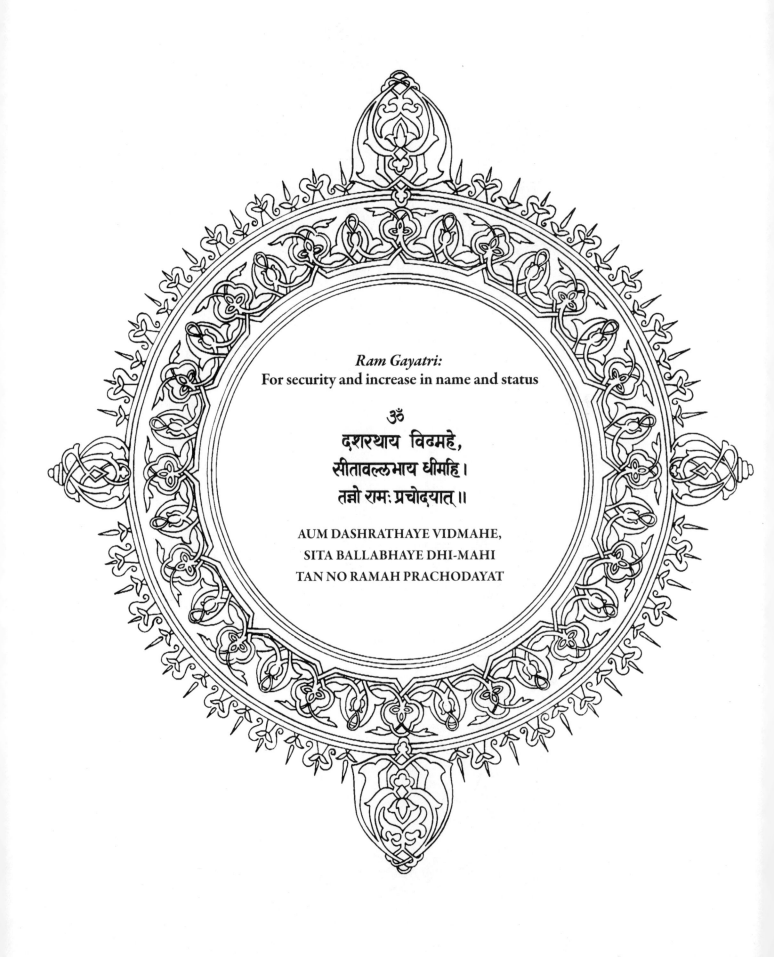

Ram Gayatri:
For security and increase in name and status

ॐ
दशरथाय विद्महे,
सीतावल्लभाय धीमहि।
तन्नो रामः प्रचोदयात्॥

AUM DASHRATHAYE VIDMAHE,
SITA BALLABHAYE DHI-MAHI
TAN NO RAMAH PRACHODAYAT

Ram

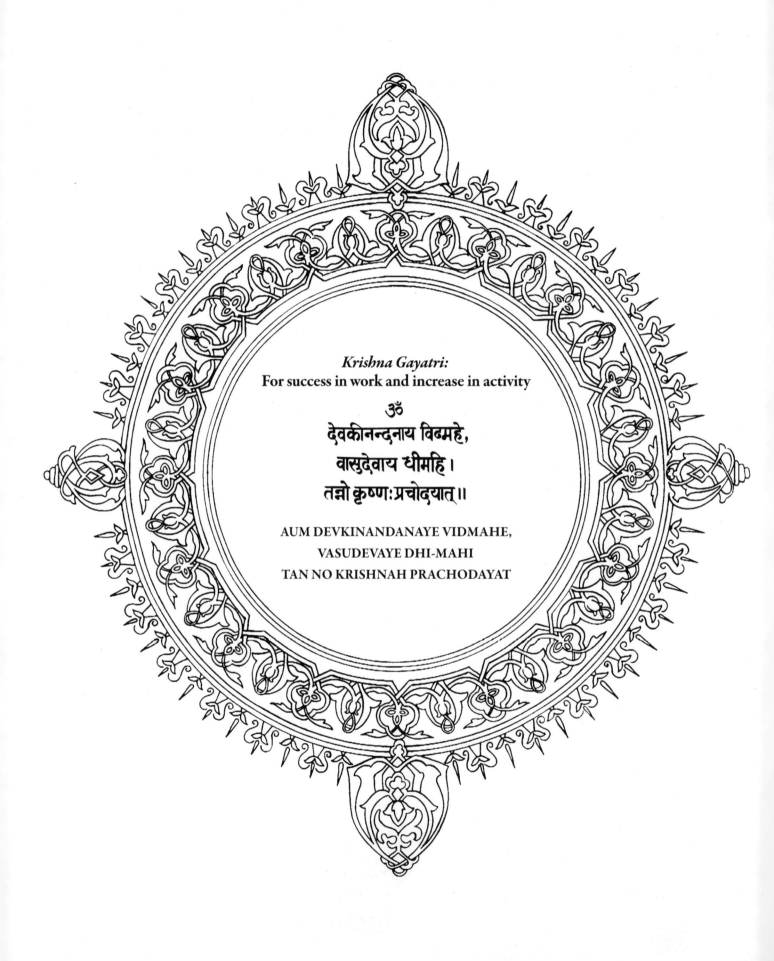

Krishna Gayatri:
For success in work and increase in activity

ॐ
देवकीनन्दनाय विद्महे,
वासुदेवाय धीमहि ।
तन्नो कृष्णः प्रचोदयात् ॥

AUM DEVKINANDANAYE VIDMAHE,
VASUDEVAYE DHI-MAHI
TAN NO KRISHNAH PRACHODAYAT

Krishna

Hanuman Gayatri:
For increasing love in performing duties and selfless service

ॐ

आञ्जनेयाय विद्महे,

महाबलाय धीमहि।

तन्नो हनुमान् प्रचोदयात्॥

AUM ANJANEYAYE VIDMAHE,

MAHABALAYE DHI-MAHI

TANNO HANUMAN PRACHODAYAT

Hanuman

Durga Gayatri:
For victory over obstacles, enemies, pains, and sufferings

ॐ
गिरिजायै विद्महे,
शिवप्रियायै धीमहि।
तन्नो दुर्गा प्रचोदयात्॥

AUM GIRJAYE VIDMAHE,
SHIV PRIYAYE DHI-MAHI
TANNO DURGA PRACHODAYAT

Durga

Lakshmi Gayatri:
For wealth, luxuries,
status, and promotion in a job

ॐ
महालक्ष्म्यै विद्महे,
विष्णुप्रियाय धीमहि।
तन्नो लक्ष्मी प्रचोदयात्॥

AUM MAHALAKSHMAYE VIDMAHE,
VISHNUPRIYAYE DHI-MAHI
TANNO LAKSHMIH PRACHODAYAT

Kamla (Lakshmi)

Saraswati Gayatri:
**For memory, wisdom,
knowledge, and creativity**

ॐ
सरस्वत्यै विद्महे ,
ब्रह्मापुऱ्यै धीमहि ।
तन्नो सरस्वती प्रचोदयात् ॥

AUM SARASWATEYE VIDMAHE,
RIYE DHI-MAHI
TANNO SARASWATI PRACHODAYAT

Mantagi (Saraswati)

Kali Mantra:
**For relieving difficulties and
fear of death and increasing love and forgiveness**

ॐ

जयन्ती मङ्गला काली भद्रकाली कपालिनी ।
दुर्गा शिवा क्षमा धात्री स्वाहा स्वधा नमोऽस्तु ते ॥

**AUM JAYANTI MANGALA KAALI
BHADRA KALI KAPALINI
DURGA KSHAMA SHIVAA DHAATRI
SVAHA SVADHA NAMO-STU-TE**

Kali

Tripura Gayatri:
**For prosperity, abundance,
and marital bliss**

ॐ

ॐ त्रिपुर सुन्दर्य विद्महे कामेश्वराय धीमिहि।
तन्नो क्लिन्ने प्रचोदयात् ॥

AUM TRIPURASUNDARYAI VIDMAHE,
KAMESHVARYAI DHI-MAHI
TANNO KLINNE PRACHODAYAT

Tripur Sundari (Shri/Shodashi)

Vishnu Gayatri:
For welfare of one's family

ॐ
पञ्चवक्त्राय विद्महे,
महादेवाय धीमहि।
तन्नो रूद्रः प्रचोदयात् ॥

AUM NARAYANAYE VIDMAHE,
VASUDEVAYE DHI-MAHI
TAN NO VISHNU PRACHODAYAT

Brahma Gayatri: **To increase productivity**

ॐ
दशरथाय विद्महे,
सीतावल्लभाय धीमहि।
तन्नो रामः प्रचोदयात् ॥

AUM PARMESHWARAYE VIDMAHE,
PARATATTVAYE DHI-MAHI
TAN NO BRAHMA PRACHODAYAT

*Ganga, born from the divine energy of Lord Vishnu,
daughter of Lord Brahma*

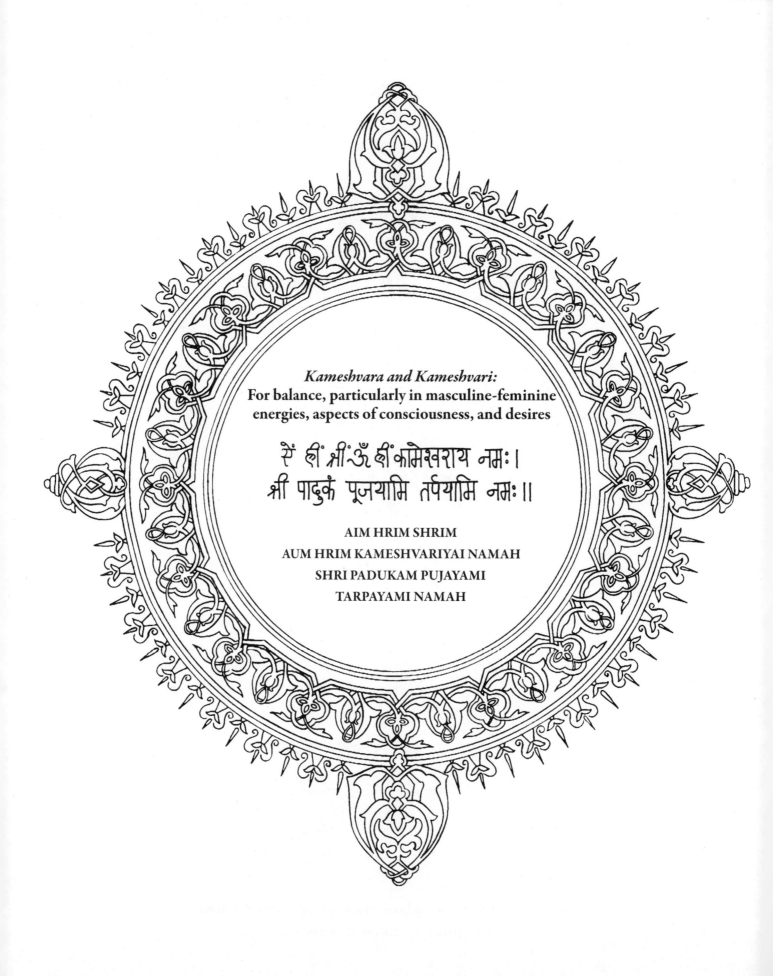

Kameshvara and Kameshvari:
**For balance, particularly in masculine-feminine
energies, aspects of consciousness, and desires**

रें ह्रीं श्रीं ॐ ह्रीं कामेश्वराय नमः ।
श्री पादुकं पूजयामि तर्पयामि नमः ॥

**AIM HRIM SHRIM
AUM HRIM KAMESHVARIYAI NAMAH
SHRI PADUKAM PUJAYAMI
TARPAYAMI NAMAH**

Kameshvara and Kameshvari

Muladhara Chakra

Svadhishthana Chakra

Manipura Chakra

Anahata Chakra

Vishuddha Chakra

Ajna Chakra

Soma Chakra

Sahasrara Chakra

THE CHAKRAS

Muladhara Chakra:
**For security, stability, awareness,
inner strength, and freedom from disease**

Muladhara Bija Seed Sound:
LANG

Muladhara Bija Petal Sound:
VANG SHANG KSHANG SANG

वं शं षं सं

Muladhara Chakra

मूलाधार चक्र

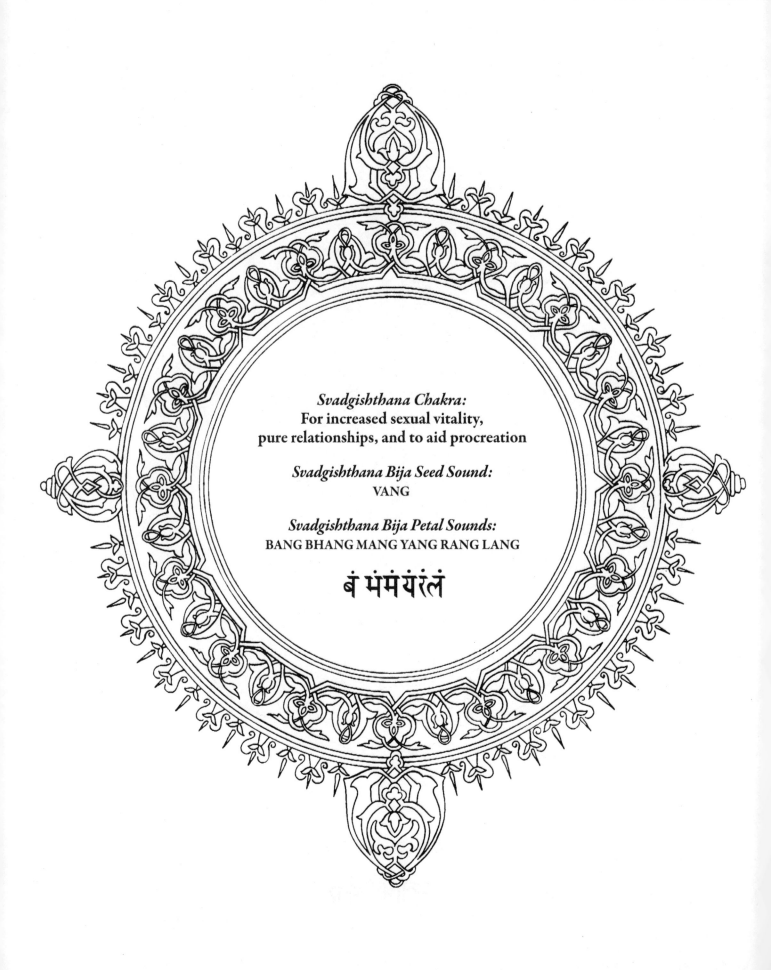

Svadgishthana Chakra:
**For increased sexual vitality,
pure relationships, and to aid procreation**

Svadgishthana Bija Seed Sound:
VANG

Svadgishthana Bija Petal Sounds:
BANG BHANG MANG YANG RANG LANG

बं भं मं यं रं लं

Svadhishthana Chakra

स्वाधिष्ठान् चक्र

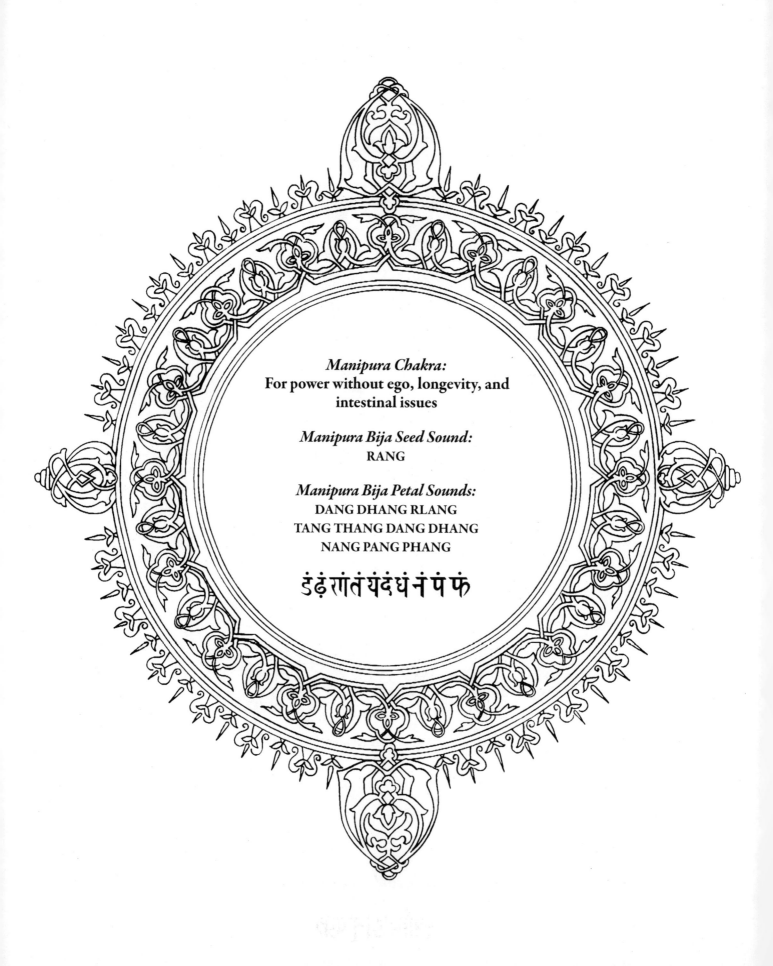

Manipura Chakra:
For power without ego, longevity, and
intestinal issues

Manipura Bija Seed Sound:
RANG

Manipura Bija Petal Sounds:
DANG DHANG RLANG
TANG THANG DANG DHANG
NANG PANG PHANG

डं ढं णं तं यं दं धं नं पं फं

Manipura Chakra

मणिपूर चक्र

Anahata Chakra: For love, balance, compassion, faith, and cardiac issues

Anahata Bija Seed Sound:
YANG

Anahata Bija Petal Sounds:
KANG KHANG GANG
GHANG YONG CANG CHANG JANG
JHANG UANG TANG THANG

कं खं गं घं ङं यं छं जं झं ञं टं ठं

Anahata Chakra

अनाहत् चक्र

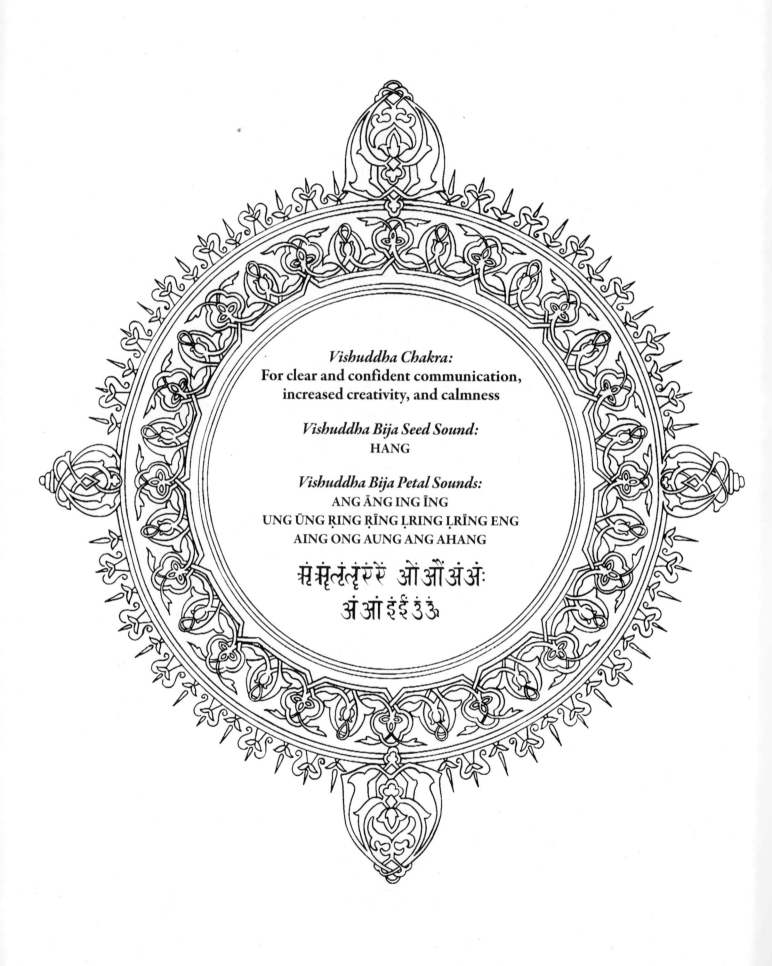

Vishuddha Chakra:
**For clear and confident communication,
increased creativity, and calmness**

Vishuddha Bija Seed Sound:
HANG

Vishuddha Bija Petal Sounds:
ANG ĀNG ING ĪNG
UNG ŪNG ṚING ṜING ḶRING ḶṚING ENG
AING ONG AUNG ANG AHANG

अं अं ऋ ॠ ऌ ॡ ए ऐ ओ औ अं अः
अं आं इ ई उ ऊ

Vishuddha Chakra

विशुद्ध चक्र

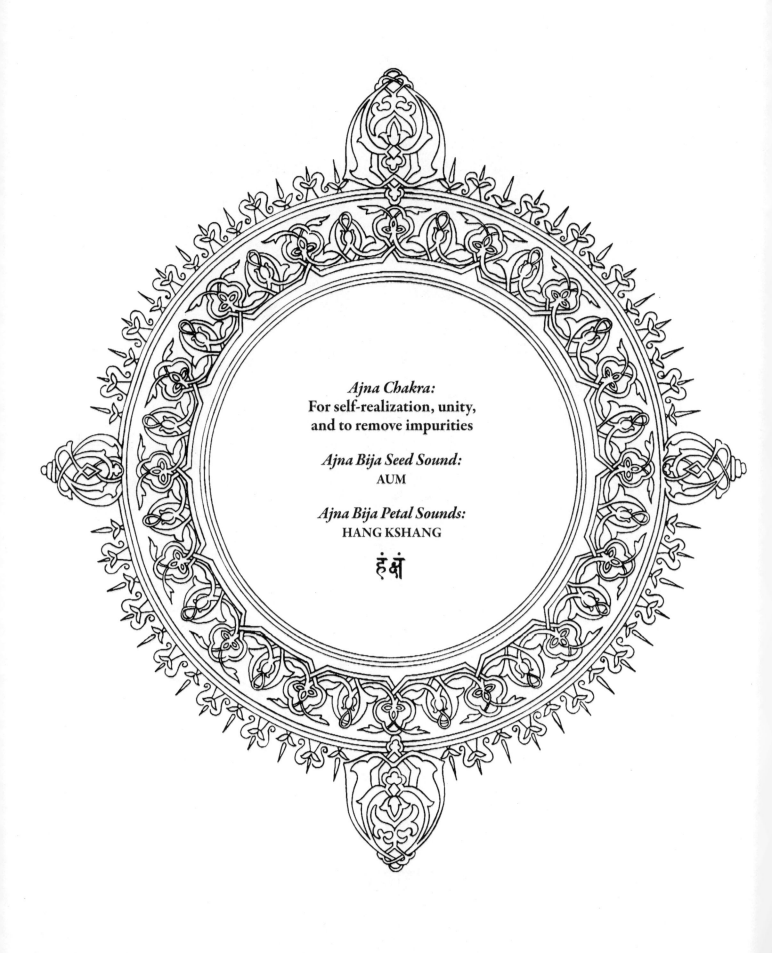

Ajna Chakra:
**For self-realization, unity,
and to remove impurities**

Ajna Bija Seed Sound:
AUM

Ajna Bija Petal Sounds:
HANG KSHANG

हं क्षं

Ajna Chakra

आज्ञा चक्र

Soma Chakra:
**To release anxiety and anger;
to become more peaceful, self-contented,
calm, and cool; and to aid eyesight**

Soma Bija Seed Sound:
AUM

ॐ

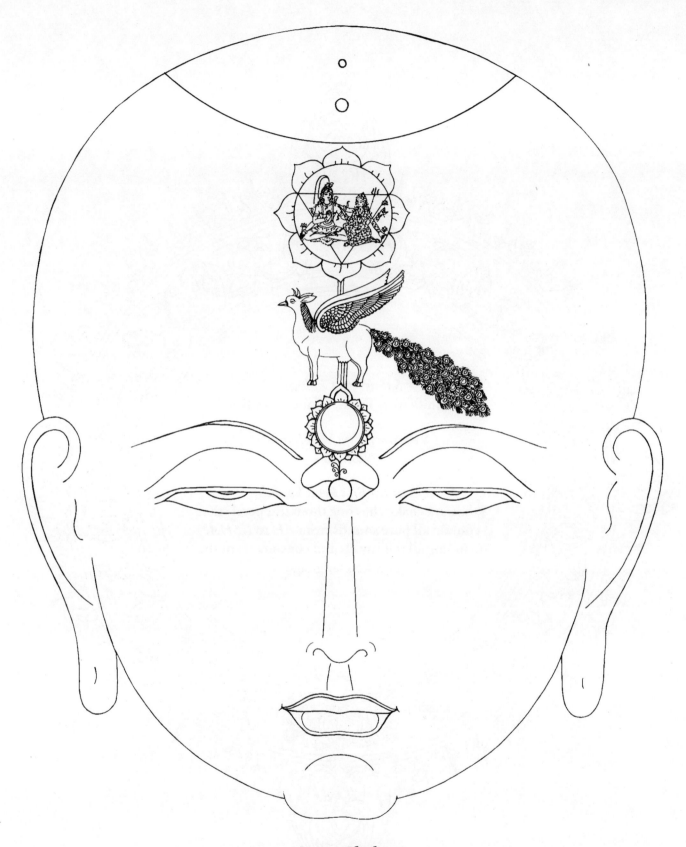

Soma Chakra

सोम चक्र

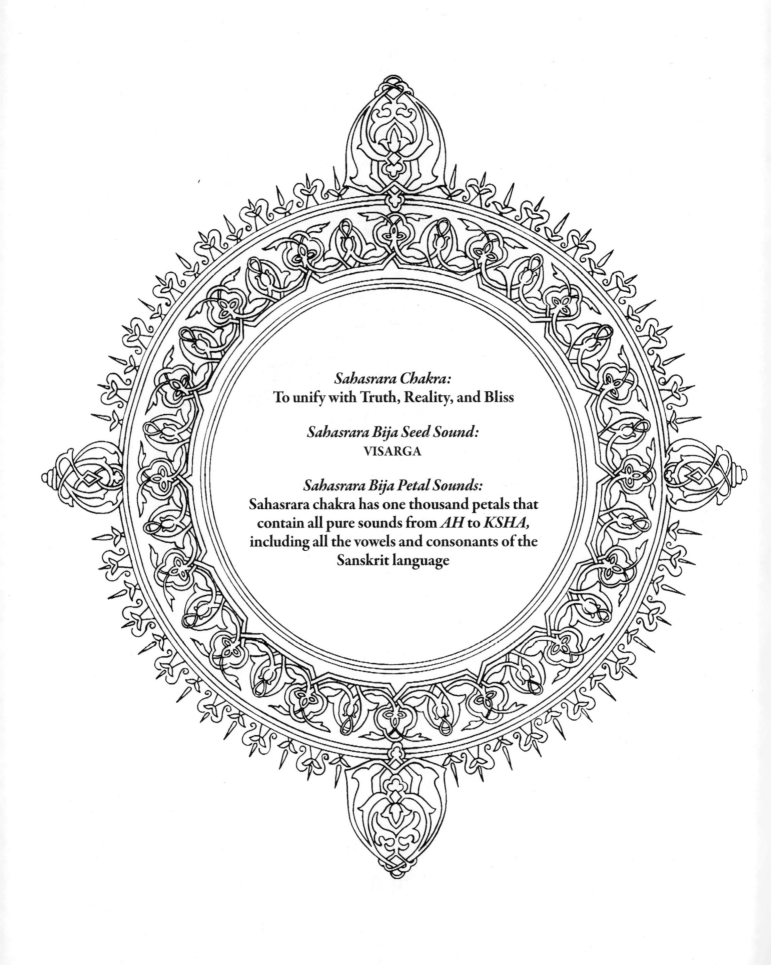

Sahasrara Chakra:
To unify with Truth, Reality, and Bliss

Sahasrara Bija Seed Sound:
VISARGA

Sahasrara Bija Petal Sounds:
Sahasrara chakra has one thousand petals that
contain all pure sounds from *AH* to *KSHA*,
including all the vowels and consonants of the
Sanskrit language

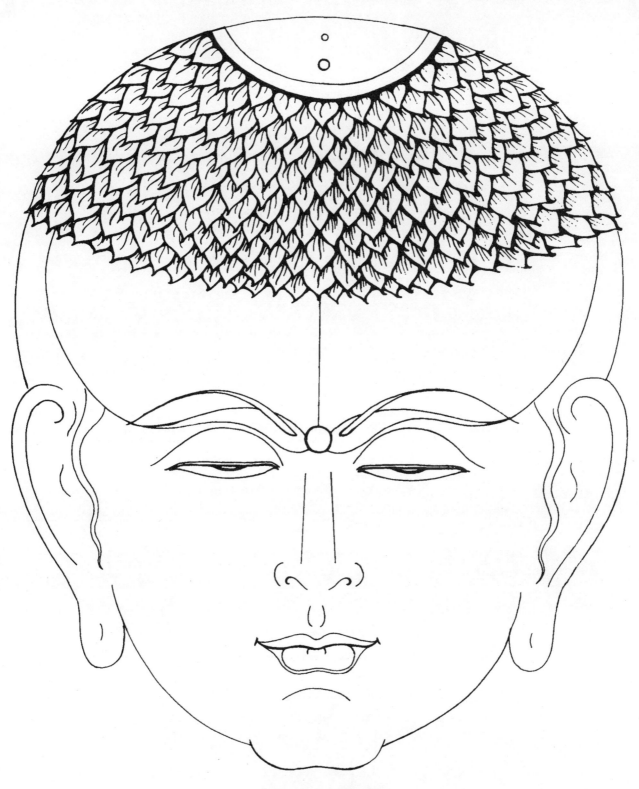

Sahasrara Chakra

सहस्रार चक्र

GANESHA YANTRA

DURGA YANTRA

KALI YANTRA

TARA YANTRA

TRIPUR SUNDARI
(SHODASHI) YANTRA

BHUVANESHWARI YANTRA

CHINNAMASTA YANTRA

TRIPUR BHAIRAVI YANTRA

BAGLA MUKHI YANTRA

MANTAGI YANTRA

SHRI (SHODASHI) YANTRA

POWER
YANTRAS

Ganesha Yantra:
To create balance and remove obstacles

GAJANANAM BHUTGANADI SEVITAM

KAPITHYA JAMBO PHALCHARU BHAKSHANAM

UMA SUTAM SHOKVINASH KARAKAM

NAMAMI VIGHNESHWAR PADPANKAJAM

GANESHA YANTRA

Durga Yantra:
For serenity and purity

AUM HRING DUNG DURGAYE NAMAH

DURGA YANTRA

Kali Yantra:
For inspiration, acceptance of others, and curing depression and pessimism

KRING KRING KRING
HING HRING DAKSHINE KALIKE
KRING KRING KRING HRING HRING
HUNG HUNG SWAHA

KALI YANTRA

Tara Yantra:
**For freedom from rules and regulations
and for inspiration**

AING AUNG HRING

KRING HUM PHAT

TARA YANTRA

Tripur Sundari (Shodashi) Yantra:
For removing fear of death and other primal fears

HRING KA AE EE
LA HRING HA SA KA HA LA
HRING SA KA LA HRING

TRIPUR SUNDARI (SHODASHI) YANTRA

Bhuvaneshwari Yantra:
For increasing consciousness and awareness

HRING

BHUVANESHWARI YANTRA

Chinnamasta Yantra:
For increasing willpower and vision

SHRING HRING KLING AING

VAJRAVAIROCHNIYE

HUNG HUNG PHAT SWAHA

CHINNAMASTA YANTRA

Tripur Bhairavi Yantra:
For overcoming sickness, doubt, and desires

HASAIN HASKARING HASAIN

TRIPUR BHAIRAVI YANTRA

Bagla Mukhi Yantra:
**For influence over others, removing obstacles,
and increasing self-confidence and independence**

**AUM HRING BAGLAMUKHI SARVA
DUSHTANAM VAVACHAMUKHAM
ISTAMBHAY JIVHAMKEELAY
BUDDHINASHAY
HRING AUM SWAHA**

BAGLA MUKHI YANTRA

Mantagi Yantra:
For increasing abilities in speech, music, writing, and creativity

**AUM HRING KLING HUM
MANTAGAIYE PHAT SWAHA**

MANTAGI YANTRA

Shri (Shodashi) Yantra:
**For dissolution of obstacles to higher
consciousness, especially fear**

**HRING KA AE EE
LA HRING HA SA KA HA LA
HRING SA KA LA HRING**

SHRI (SHODASHI) YANTRA

Sun

Moon

Mars

Mercury

Jupiter

Venus

Saturn

**Rahu,
North Node of the Moon**

**Ketu,
South Node of the Moon**

THE PLANETS

Sun Mantra:
**For influencing the intellect and
increasing assertiveness, extroversion,
and exuberance**

☉

AUM HRIM

HANSA SUIRIYAYE

NAMAH AUM

Sun

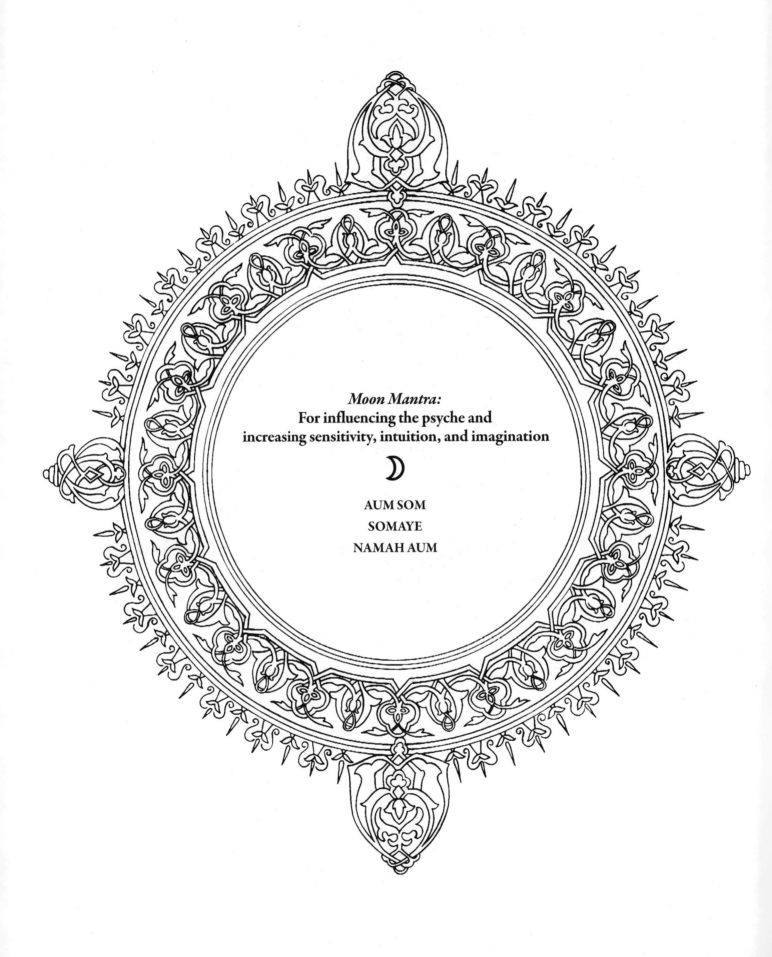

Moon Mantra:
**For influencing the psyche and
increasing sensitivity, intuition, and imagination**

**AUM SOM
SOMAYE
NAMAH AUM**

Moon

Mars Mantra:
**For influencing behavior and increasing courage,
patience, and self-confidence**

♂

AUM BHAUM

BHAUMAYE

NAMAH AUM

Mars

Mercury Mantra:
For quick wit, cunning, youthfulness, and humor

☿

AUM BUM

BUDHAYE

NAMAH AUM

Mercury

Jupiter Mantra:
For self-illumination, mental energy, and knowledge

2⌉

AUM BRIM

BRAHASPATAYE

NAMAH AUM

Jupiter

Venus Mantra:
**For increased sexual pleasure,
passion, and sensuousness**

♀

AUM SHUM

SHUKRAYE

NAMAH AUM

Venus

Saturn Mantra:
**For increased wisdom, sense of justice,
and leadership abilities**

♄

**AUM SHAM
SHANAISHCHARAYE
NAMAH AUM**

Saturn

Rahu Mantra:
**For mental influence,
especially for artistic endeavors and writing**

**AUM RAM
RAHUVE
NAMAH AUM**

Rahu, North Node of the Moon

Ketu Mantra:
**For nonattachment and
increased spirituality and healing abilities**

AUM KAIM

KETAVE

NAMAH AUM

Ketu, South Node of the Moon

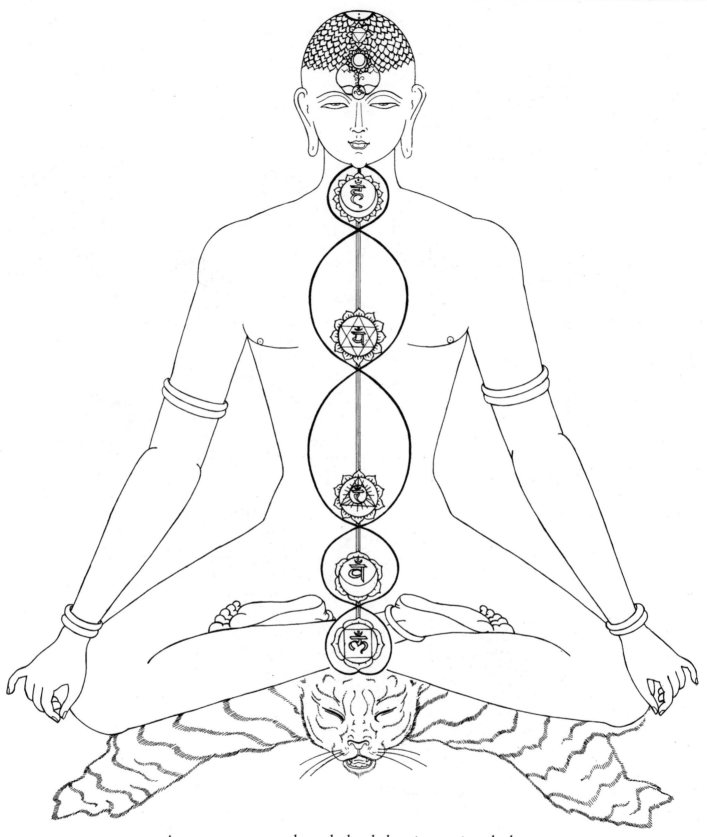

As energy moves up through the chakras it energizes the latent desires of those chakras. When the energy reaches the seventh chakra, we are beyond desire. This is the dwelling place of enlightened beings, the seat of the self or individual consciousness.